Context Disclaimer

This book discusses payment systems, financial infrastructure, and real-world use cases involving cryptocurrencies, digital settlement, and alternative methods of exchange. Its purpose is explanatory, not prescriptive. The material presented is intended to describe how systems function in practice, particularly where access, permission, and settlement diverge from common assumptions. It does not advocate for any specific course of action, product, platform, or financial strategy.

Nothing in this book constitutes legal, financial, medical, tax, or regulatory advice. No statements should be interpreted as guidance on how to comply with, avoid, or challenge laws, regulations, contractual obligations, or institutional policies. Examples involving payment processors, banks, cryptocurrencies, or other financial tools are provided solely to illustrate operational behaviors and system dynamics. They are not endorsements, recommendations, or instructions.

References to cryptocurrencies, digital assets, precious metals, barter, or direct exchange are presented in an informational context. These references are used to demonstrate how different settlement mechanisms function under varying conditions, including scenarios where traditional intermediaries restrict or delay access. Such references should not be interpreted as investment advice or as a suggestion that any asset class is suitable for any particular individual or situation.

The author makes no representations regarding the legality, suitability, or risk profile of any technology, asset, or method discussed. Laws, regulations, and enforcement practices vary by jurisdiction and are subject to change. Readers are solely responsible for understanding and complying with all applicable local, state, national, and international laws, regulations, and contractual obligations relevant to their activities.

This book is written from an operational and analytical perspective. Its focus is on system behavior, incentive structures, and real-world outcomes, not ideology, prediction, or persuasion. The intent is to improve understanding of how financial and payment systems operate under constraint so that readers can think more clearly about risk, dependency, and resilience within their own legal and ethical boundaries.

Operating Without Approval

Operating
Without Approval

Gary Haywood

Introduction

Operating in Conditional Systems

This book is not a manifesto, forecast, or protest. It is an operational examination of how modern systems behave when permission quietly replaces settlement. That distinction matters because most people do not experience system failure as a dramatic collapse. They experience it as friction, delay, denial, or silence. Accounts remain visible but unusable. Balances exist but cannot be accessed. Rules are not broken; they are reinterpreted. Nothing appears wrong, until nothing works.

Conditional systems are defined by this gap between appearance and function. On the surface, commerce continues as usual. Beneath it, access is contingent. Settlement is no longer guaranteed; it is granted. The difference is subtle, but the consequences are decisive. When permission replaces settlement, the system no longer exists to complete transactions, it exists to manage risk, reputation, and exposure for intermediaries. The operator absorbs the uncertainty.

Most individuals and small businesses do not design for this reality because they are not taught to see it. Financial life is framed as a matter of compliance, participation, and trust in infrastructure. The assumption is that lawful activity ensures continuity. In practice, legality is often irrelevant. What matters is category risk, algorithmic thresholds, and internal policy, none of which are transparent or negotiable. Understanding this is not pessimism. It is situational awareness.

This volume applies that same discipline to payment systems, currency design, and measurement errors that shape everyday survival for individuals and small operators. It does not argue that modern systems are malicious or destined to fail. It observes that they are optimized for institutional risk management, not individual continuity. Once that is understood, behavior can adjust accordingly.

The goal of this book is clarity. Not alarm. Not advocacy. Clarity about where permission exists, where it does not, and how that boundary affects real-world outcomes. When settlement is final, planning is possible. When settlement is conditional, resilience must be designed upstream.

Operating better begins with seeing the system as it is.

Chapter 1   The Gatekeepers You Don't See

Most businesses do not fail because demand disappears. Customers still want the product. The service is still needed. The operator is still willing and able to deliver. What fails first is settlement. Payment stops moving, not because a transaction is illegal or fraudulent, but because permission is withdrawn. When that happens, the business does not wind down gradually, it stalls abruptly.

Payment processors sit quietly between buyers and sellers, largely unnoticed during normal operation. They are designed to be invisible. Transactions clear. Funds settle. Statements reconcile. This invisibility creates the impression that payment is a neutral utility, like electricity or water. It is not. Payment is conditional access to a privately governed network, and that access can be restricted at any time.

When restriction occurs, it rarely arrives with a clear explanation. An account is flagged. A reserve is imposed. Settlement timelines stretch from days to weeks, then to indefinite. Funds are frozen pending "review." Communication becomes generic, slow, or nonexistent. There is no court order. No formal accusation. No meaningful appeals process. The operator is informed only that a decision has been made in accordance with internal policy.

Risk policy overrides legality. This is a critical distinction. Payment processors are not tasked with determining whether activity is lawful; they are tasked with minimizing exposure, to charge backs, regulatory scrutiny, reputational risk, and uncertainty. A business can be fully compliant and still be categorized as high risk. Association, product type, transaction pattern, or volume changes can trigger restrictions without warning. The burden of proof falls entirely on the operator, and the standards for reinstatement are opaque.

Once payment becomes conditional, commerce becomes optional. Payroll obligations do not pause. Rent does not adjust. Inventory remains owed. The business continues to incur costs even as revenue access is constrained. This asymmetry is the quiet failure mode of modern commerce. From the outside, nothing appears broken. From the inside, the system is no longer functional.

This dynamic is not limited to fringe industries or marginal operators. Entire lawful sectors operate under constant exposure to payment interruption. The risk is structural, not behavioral. The more centralized and permission-ed the payment layer becomes, the more fragile commerce becomes beneath it.

Cryptocurrency did not emerge to replace money. It emerged to remove this permission layer. Its core function is not speculation, ideology, or disruption. It is final settlement without approval. Bitcoin does not evaluate the transaction. It does not score risk. It does not reverse payment. It does not freeze funds. It settles.

That single property, irreversible settlement without intermediary permission, is why this technology exists and why it continues to be used long after speculative cycles fade. It is not an escape from responsibility or law. It is a response to a system where access to commerce can be revoked without recourse.

This book is about understanding that distinction. Not to reject existing systems, but to see them clearly. Because once payment requires approval, survival depends on knowing who holds the switch, and what happens when it is turned off.

Chapter 2   When Currency Stops, Reality Starts

Digital currency functions only while infrastructure holds. It depends on uninterrupted power, stable networks, functioning intermediaries, and institutional permission. As long as those layers remain intact, balances appear reliable and access feels permanent. The moment one layer fails, currency does not degrade gradually, it becomes inert. Numbers still exist on screens, but their ability to move disappears.

Bank holidays, payment outages, cyber incidents, and administrative freezes expose this reality quickly. Transactions stall. Cards decline. ATMs empty. Customer support scripts replace resolution. In those moments, the distinction between *having money* and *accessing money* becomes unavoidable. The system does not ask how much you have. It asks whether the rails are open.

Historically and practically, this window is short. Confidence erodes faster than infrastructure recovers. Within days, not months, the dominant question shifts from account balance to possession. What do you physically control that others will recognize as exchangeable? Access becomes less relevant than custody. This transition is not theoretical. It is a recurring pattern whenever centralized systems pause, even briefly.

Under normal conditions, digital abstraction is efficient. It reduces friction, increases speed, and simplifies accounting. Under stress, abstraction becomes a liability. The more layers required to authorize and complete a transaction, the more points of failure exist. When one layer pauses, the entire structure stalls. The system is not broken; it is behaving exactly as designed.

This dynamic mirrors the operational lessons explored in *Mastering the Basics*. Fundamentals matter most when systems fail. Complexity performs well in stable environments and collapses under strain. Simple, direct mechanisms persist longer because they require fewer permissions to function. This is not nostalgia for older systems; it is recognition of how dependency chains behave under pressure.

Preparedness, in this context, is not ideology. It is not pessimism or speculation. It is acknowledgment of how systems actually behave when stressed. Preparing for access constraints does not imply distrust in institutions; it reflects an understanding that institutions prioritize systemic stability over individual continuity. Their mandate is to manage aggregate risk, not personal outcomes.

The mistake many people make is assuming that disruption will announce itself clearly. It rarely does. More often, it arrives as inconvenience, delay, or temporary restriction, each individually tolerable, collectively paralyzing. By the time the situation is recognized as serious, options have narrowed.

This chapter does not argue that digital systems are failing or obsolete. It argues that they are conditional. When those conditions are unmet, reality asserts itself quickly. Planning that ignores this behavior is fragile. Planning that accounts for it is simply realistic.

When currency stops moving, reality does not change. It becomes visible.

C hapter 3   Purity Becomes the Language

When systems pause, branding fades. Logos, stamps, and institutional promises lose relevance because they depend on functioning verification networks. In constrained environments, trust shifts away from authority and toward substance. What matters is not who issued the object, but what it is made of, how it can be verified, and whether it performs its function without explanation.

This is why purity, weight, and direct verifiability replace symbols when settlement systems stall. Measurements become the language. A stated purity .999 fine silver or .9999 fine gold, is not a brand claim. It is a specification. It communicates value without requiring belief in an issuer, a logo, or a governing body. The metal does not argue for itself. It either meets the standard or it does not.

Under normal conditions, stamps, seals, and hallmarks are useful. They reduce transaction costs by signaling authenticity within established systems. Under disruption, those same markers become secondary. Their meaning depends on shared confidence in the system that issued them. When that confidence weakens, the underlying substance carries the transaction.

This is why unmarked or minimally marked bars often outperform ornate pieces in constrained settings. Decoration introduces questions. Questions introduce delay. Delay introduces friction. A plain bar of known purity shortens negotiation because it reduces the number of assumptions required. Weight can be measured. Purity can be tested. The transaction can proceed without explanation.

This behavior is not unique to precious metals. It reflects a broader operational principle: in stressed systems, people trade what they can verify directly. Anything that requires interpretation, trust in authority, or third-party confirmation is discounted. The simpler the verification process, the more resilient the exchange.

This principle scales beyond metals and money. Systems that rely on multiple permissions, endorsements, or reputational layers perform well in stable environments and degrade rapidly under stress. Systems that preserve function with fewer dependencies persist longer. Reducing dependency is not an aesthetic choice; it is a resilience strategy.

Increasing verifiability does not mean rejecting institutions or complexity outright. It means recognizing which components are essential and which are decorative. When conditions are favorable, decoration is harmless. When conditions tighten, decoration becomes drag.

Purity becomes the language because it compresses trust into measurable form. It removes the need for narrative, authority, or branding. It allows exchange to continue when symbols no longer speak.

The lesson is not about hoarding metal or predicting collapse. It is about understanding how value communicates under constraint. Preserve function. Reduce explanation. Design systems that speak for themselves when everything else goes quiet.

C hapter 4   Currency Is Infinite. Money Is Not.

Currency is expandable; human effort is not. Time, attention, skill, and physical energy are finite inputs. When an unconstrained unit is used to measure constrained labor, distortion is inevitable. This distortion does not require bad intent, corruption, or conspiracy. It emerges automatically from design. The system behaves exactly as its measurements allow.

Currency functions well as a medium of exchange and an accounting layer. It moves value efficiently and enables coordination at scale. The problem arises when currency is treated as a stable store of value rather than a flexible unit of account. When expansion is discretionary, the unit itself changes while the effort it measures does not. The result is a mismatch between input and outcome.

This is not a moral failure. It is a mechanical one. A broken ruler cannot produce accurate measurements, no matter how carefully it is used. If the ruler stretches unpredictably, disciplined behavior yields inconsistent results. Perfect effort does not guarantee proportional reward because the measuring tool is unstable.

Savings dilute not because saving is wrong, but because the unit in which savings are measured is adjustable. Patience is mispriced because time is rewarded less than immediacy in an expanding system. Leverage is rewarded not because it is prudent, but because it accelerates exposure to expanding units. These outcomes are not policy mistakes; they are predictable consequences.

This is why disciplined individuals often feel as though they are falling behind despite doing everything "correctly." The inputs are sound. The behavior is consistent. The results drift. Frustration follows, not because effort failed, but because measurement shifted. Without understanding this, people internalize systemic distortion as personal failure.

The Learning Curve examines what happens when individuals recognize this misalignment. The moment the measurement error becomes visible, behavior changes. People stop optimizing for approval within the system and begin optimizing for preservation across time. The curve is not about rejection; it is about recalibration.

Adaptation takes many forms. Some reduce exposure to currency-based measurement. Others seek assets or structures with enforced scarcity. Others simplify obligations and reduce leverage. These are not ideological choices. They are rational responses to unstable measurement.

Understanding the distinction between currency and money does not require abandoning modern systems. It requires recognizing their limits. Currency excels at movement. Money excels at preservation. Confusing the two corrupts both functions.

The goal is not certainty. It is alignment. When effort is measured with a stable unit, discipline compounds. When the ruler is broken, discipline erodes. Seeing the difference is the first step toward operating better within imperfect systems.

Chapter 5   Discipline Inside a Distorted Ruler

Disciplined individuals often feel penalized not because discipline has stopped working, but because the measuring unit has shifted beneath them. The behaviors that once produced reliable outcomes, saving, planning, avoiding excess risk, still function, but their results appear muted or delayed. The effort is real. The discipline is intact. What has changed is the frame used to evaluate progress.

When currency expansion outpaces effort, long-term planning becomes fragile. Goals set in nominal terms drift. Benchmarks lose meaning. Time horizons compress. People who think in years or decades find themselves competing with systems optimized for immediacy. This creates a psychological pressure to abandon discipline in favor of speed, leverage, or speculation, not because those behaviors are superior, but because they appear to be rewarded.

The danger is not miscalculation; it is misinterpretation. Without understanding measurement distortion, disciplined individuals conclude that restraint is obsolete or that the system is rigged against them personally. This emotional framing leads to reactive decisions. Discipline erodes not because it fails, but because it is misunderstood.

Recognizing distortion changes the response. Once the ruler is identified as unstable, outcomes are reinterpreted correctly. Slow progress is no longer read as failure. Preservation becomes visible again. The objective shifts from outperforming an expanding unit to maintaining coherence across time. This reframing restores control.

Structure is the antidote. Structure in obligations. Structure in exposure. Structure in decision-making. When measurement is unstable, structure limits damage and preserves optionality. This principle appears repeatedly across *Mastering the Basics* and *The Power of No Debt*: reduce variables, constrain risk, and operate within what can be controlled.

Outrage offers no leverage. Emotional reactions consume energy without altering the system. They feel justified, but they do not restore agency. Structure does. Clear boundaries, conservative assumptions, and reduced dependency allow disciplined behavior to compound quietly, even when public metrics suggest otherwise.

Operating inside a distorted ruler requires patience and clarity. It means accepting that external signals may be misleading while internal coherence remains intact. The goal is not to win a race measured incorrectly, but to remain functional long enough for conditions to change or for better measurement to emerge.

Discipline still works. It simply works differently when the ruler is broken.

Chapter 6 — Predictable Adaptation, Not Rebellion

When trust erodes, rational people adapt. They do not need ideology, slogans, or collective movements to do so. Adaptation occurs quietly, incrementally, and often without coordination. Individuals adjust behavior to preserve effort, reduce exposure, and maintain continuity. This is not rebellion. It is system response.

History shows that when measurement becomes unstable and access becomes conditional, people migrate toward structures that offer durability. They seek mechanisms that function with fewer permissions, fewer intermediaries, and clearer rules. The motivation is not opposition to existing systems, but reliability when those systems impose friction or uncertainty.

Bitcoin, capped assets, and direct exchange fit this pattern. They are not revolutions in the political sense. They do not require mass adoption to be useful. They operate as parallel settlement mechanisms that function when approval is absent and finality matters. Their appeal is not novelty; it is predictability.

Final settlement changes behavior. When a transaction cannot be reversed, frozen, or delayed by a third party, planning becomes possible again. Risk is clearer. Obligations are symmetrical. This does not eliminate responsibility, it enforces it. Mistakes are borne directly, not redistributed through abstraction. For disciplined operators, this clarity is preferable to conditional convenience.

This logic aligns directly with the principles outlined in *The Power of No Debt*. Leverage magnifies fragility in systems where settlement is uncertain. When access can be revoked, obligations become one-sided: debts remain enforceable while receivables are conditional. Avoiding leverage is not moral conservatism; it is exposure management.

Direct exchange and capped systems reduce this asymmetry. They shorten the distance between action and consequence. They eliminate layers that exist primarily to manage institutional risk at the expense of individual continuity. In doing so, they restore a degree of agency, not freedom from law or responsibility, but freedom from silent dependency.

It is important to distinguish adaptation from advocacy. Using alternative settlement mechanisms does not imply rejection of existing institutions. Most people continue to operate within traditional systems while selectively reducing points of failure. This hybrid approach is common because it is practical. Systems are used where they work and bypassed where they introduce unnecessary risk.

Adaptation is rarely loud. It does not announce itself as a movement. It shows up in behavior: reduced leverage, diversified settlement options, simplified obligations, and an emphasis on finality. These changes accumulate quietly, driven by experience rather than belief.

This chapter does not argue that one system will replace another. It observes that when approval becomes conditional and measurement unstable, alternatives emerge naturally. Predictable adaptation follows predictable pressure.

The outcome is not collapse. It is migration.

Epilogue

Operating Better, Not Louder

This book was never meant to stand alone. It exists within a broader operating framework that runs through all of my work. Each book addresses a different layer of the same problem: how to remain functional, disciplined, and coherent inside systems that are imperfect, conditional, and often misaligned with individual effort.

Mastering the Basics begins at the foundation. It is about controllables, habits, structure, repetition, and discipline that hold when motivation fades or conditions deteriorate. Its core argument is simple: when systems become unreliable, fundamentals matter more, not less. The principles in that book are the baseline for surviving any environment where outcomes cannot be assumed.

The Learning Curve addresses what happens next. It focuses on adaptation when effort and results diverge. When the rules shift quietly, disciplined people often experience confusion before clarity. That book explains how to recognize distortion, recalibrate expectations, and continue forward without internalizing systemic failure as personal inadequacy. It is about reading curvature instead of forcing straight lines through bent systems.

The Power of No Debt moves the framework into risk management. It examines leverage, obligation, and asymmetry. In a world where settlement can be delayed or denied, debt amplifies vulnerability. That book is not anti-growth; it is pro-survivability. It argues that optionality is preserved by minimizing obligations that assume continuous access and stable measurement.

Operating Without Approval fits between and around these ideas. It addresses the infrastructure layer, payment systems, currency design, and settlement mechanics that quietly shape what is possible. It explains why discipline alone is insufficient if the rails beneath it are conditional. It clarifies why some systems fail without warning and why adaptation tends to be quiet, practical, and incremental rather than ideological.

Together, these books are not a philosophy. They are an operating model.

They do not promise protection from risk or immunity from failure. They aim to reduce avoidable fragility. They emphasize clarity over comfort, structure over outrage, and understanding over optimism. The throughline is consistent: you cannot control systems, but you can control how you operate within them.

The modern environment rewards speed, leverage, and abstraction, until it doesn't. When conditions change, those same traits become liabilities. The operators who persist are rarely the loudest or most aggressive. They are the ones who understand fundamentals, recognize distortion, manage exposure, and adapt without drama.

This is not about escaping systems. It is about seeing them clearly.

Operating better does not mean feeling better. It means making fewer assumptions, reducing dependency, and preserving function when conditions tighten. That approach is not fashionable, but it is durable.

And durability, in the end, is what survives.